For Linda
Best Wishes

2020 –

design
Louise Brody

ISBN: 9781788840743

British Library Cataloguing-in-Publication Data
A catalogue record for this book is available from the British Library

The author and publisher gratefully acknowledge the permission granted to reproduce
the copyright material in this book. Every effort has been made to trace copyright
holders and to obtain their permission for the use of copyright material. The publisher
apologises for any errors or omissions in the text and would be grateful if notified of
any corrections that should be incorporated in future reprints or editions of this book.

Printed in Belgium for ACC Art Books Ltd., Woodbridge, Suffolk, England

www.accartbooks.com

ACC
ART
BOOKS

out of the blue

text
Amanda Back

special photography
James Merrell

ACC ART BOOKS

Writing the introduction for a book that celebrates half a century of my work is a distinctly powerful, thoughtful and touching sensation. I am struck by how perfectly appropriate the title *Out of the Blue* actually is. My story did indeed come 'out of the blue'! Looking back, however, the seeds of my career were present from the beginning.

Some of my earliest memories are of colour. My grandparents were very keen gardeners and, as a child, I would often garden with them. I distinctly remember one sunny spring day, looking up through the lilac flowers of their wisteria, the sharp acidic green of the first leaves, to an endless blue sky, and being genuinely touched by its beauty. I have always felt a very strong connection with nature and remain as inspired by the landscape and what I see now, as I was then.

My parents were artistic and forward-thinking; our home contemporary and filled with Heal's furniture from the 1950s, black and white fabrics and a vivid turquoise geo carpet. I was fastidious about my bedroom, the colours and patterns. My destiny was already becoming clear.

Whilst designing houses with Robin Guild in the late 1960s, I felt rather limited by the available fabrics. I was forever searching for a different language. My first trip to India was totally inspiring. The colours, landscape, dignity, architecture and soul touched my heart.

The first collection of fabric and wallpaper was called *Village*, inspired by Indian block prints yet totally reinterpreted in a vivid colour palette that was both decorative and contemporary. I felt strongly that this style of decoration needed to be shown as a lifestyle and, with that in mind, opened the first Designers Guild store in Chelsea, on London's famous King's Road. I covered sofas, had cushions made, accessorised with Clarice Cliff ceramics and vintage furniture, and so the full story began.

I had no idea how this extraordinary journey would unfold. I did, however, have determination and passion. Visual arts, theatre, opera, architecture and my travels around the world have infused my vision. Italy – its architecture, Renaissance painting and landscape, gardening, and the growing and cooking of food – have always filled my life and my work with inspiration.

Creatively and artistically I had a clear vision of what I wanted to achieve. However, running a company is not simply a creative endeavour; finance, management and production are incredibly demanding. I was a busy young mother and when I reflect upon what motivated me, it was perseverance and a total wish to be independent that propelled me to try with all my being to succeed ... to paint my own canvas.

That determination burns very deeply within me. I acknowledge that I am indeed a perfectionist and a detail-driven person. I think it is my resolve and determination that most define me. I am forever in search of the moment when the fabric, the piece of furniture – whatever I am working on – touches my soul, strikes the note; then we can launch. The challenge and the internal search are constant.

The 1970s and '80s were not easy times to be a young woman in business and I needed to work extremely hard for Designers Guild to survive and flourish. As the company started to grow, we began to export, selling to stores and designers throughout the world. Our very first exhibition was in Paris in 1978.

I steadily began to build a team. Teamwork is essential, and collaboration, care and respect for that team is fundamental. I was fortunate – and remain very fortunate – to work with incredible and like-minded people, whose energy, drive and commitment match and enhance my own.

In the mid 1980s the company was flourishing, and I knew that I needed additional expertise to take the company to the next level. I therefore invited Simon Jeffreys, my brother, to join me, bringing his experience in corporate finance. Together, we built the Designers Guild ethos.

Inspiration in many forms. FROM TOP: fashion from Christian Dior; a flowered arch in Portugal; the architecture of Luis Barragán; antique silk scarves in Tokyo.

The company remains a family business to this day. In the early 1990s, Lisa Guild, my daughter, joined the team and brought her artistic and academic expertise to the company.

With Simon by my side and with our brilliant team, we continue to build Designers Guild in the UK and across the globe. It is an innovative and creative place of work that truly values the team, their achievements, the service that we offer. We strive for excellence on all levels.

I lead – and am passionate about – every aspect of our creative endeavours. The direction of each season's collections of fabric and wallpaper, of each thread colour, of printing and weaving techniques, for all of our products including furniture, paint, bedlinen, rugs and home accessories – all are vital to the future. I am totally and passionately involved with our photography each season, which expresses the essence and image of each collection. I am also devoted to publishing books, as they hopefully inspire others and describe my journey, offering readers my inner thoughts.

Designers Guild stores continue to showcase a total lifestyle, combining our own products with other specifically curated contemporary and vintage furniture, ceramics and more. We maintain my original starting point – our interior design service both in the UK and abroad.

I am not a nostalgic person; rather, I prefer to live in the present and look to the future. I am therefore truly touched and honoured that my vision and our company are being celebrated in this book.

I hope that a message of creativity, determination, hard work and innovation will be discovered and, above all, the joy and happiness that accompany my journey, which began, quite simply, 'out of the blue'…

TRICIA GUILD

FROM TOP: frescoes by Perugino; detail of a ceramic vase; a frescoed ceiling in Italy; a contemporary chair by Marni. #11

an unconventional approach

PRECEDING PAGES: the launch of the Designers Guild Homestore, 1996. THIS PAGE: Tricia Guild in Kaffe Fassett knitwear, photographed with the *Geranium* collection, 1976.

The year is 1970 and it is the dawning of a brand-new decade – following hot on the heels of the ground-breaking cultural revolution and wild optimism of the '60s. Robin Guild and his wife, Tricia Guild, were well-known London interior designers, operating from Robin's 'Interiors' shop in Hampstead, where their clients numbered many of the movers and shakers of the day. They were fast gaining a reputation for being designers to watch and their work was lauded for its mix of modernity and innate good taste.

The Guilds made it their business to know every creative outpost in the city. One of the places they discovered was a small store belonging to David Bishop, a New Zealander who had cut his teeth at David Hicks' interior design practice. Bishop had set up his own decorating company on King's Road in Chelsea, an area that had a less than salubrious reputation at the time. Bishop, on the other hand, was known among the cognoscenti as a man of exceptional taste and style. The Guilds would often visit the store, using his furniture and accessories in their design schemes for clients.

Tricia was particularly taken with a small collection of early block prints that Bishop had brought back from a recent trip to India. Small-scale designs, rather earthy in colour and hand-printed on raw cotton, they had an engaging charm and she would use them regularly in interior projects. Following Bishop's somewhat untimely death, his business was put up for sale. The Guilds decided to buy the company, relocating to Chelsea, where they were joined by Bishop's young designer, Chris Halsey, a graduate of Hull Traders, a company known for the production of interesting and innovative fabrics. The new venture that would become Designers Guild had launched.

Using and specifying Bishop's Indian prints had inspired the young Tricia Guild, and her fascination with textiles, wallpapers and pattern began to flourish. Whilst she was enamoured with the scale and simplicity of the designs, she found the colours dull and a little dreary so she considered how she might reinvent them to create something fresher, clearer and more contemporary. The original designs had been hand-printed in India but Guild instinctively knew that this would not be commercially viable for their business. So, without any formal training, she tentatively began to feel her way and, with Halsey's help, set about creating her own design language. They found a small screen-printing business that was based on an island in the middle of the River Thames, where the craftsmen agreed to produce small print runs of up to 30 metres. Carefully and with a discipline for which she would later become known, Guild put together a small collection of fabrics based on block prints but reinvented and reinvigorated in clear, fresh colours.

FROM TOP: Designers Guild shopfront, 1977; the interior of 271 King's Road, 1977; Tricia Guild, 1977; Tricia Guild at home in London, 1978.   # 17

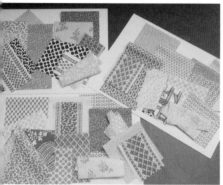

Guild was taking the company in a very different direction to the prevailing looks and styles of the moment, although she was, perhaps, naively unaware of it at the time. Heal's were promoting a revival of art nouveau and art deco patterns while Sanderson were creating perfectly matched fabrics and papers in easy neutrals and mid tones, and the key looks of the moment were classic chintzes and florals shown in a traditional sense. Most brands would show fabrics in swatch books or long lengths, and furniture and accessories would be shown in different departments, largely in isolation from the other components that would create an interior.

Trusting her instincts, Guild knew that she had to show people how to use these textiles and papers; she had to create a lifestyle that would inspire but also, crucially, reassure potential customers. Taking over a small corner of the shop (now relocated to 277 King's Road), she re-covered a sofa, had curtains made, papered the walls with her new designs and filled a pine dresser with Clarice Cliff ceramics. She added lampshades, cushions and accessories – recreating her vision of an ideal home in a shop window. The result was an immediate success and Designers Guild was later credited in *Design* magazine as being 'primarily responsible for initiating [a] revival of shopping interest in the lower end of King's Road – now a centre for leading design entrepreneurs in London.' Within a few hundred yards of the shop, Osborne & Little, Tamesa Fabrics and Habitat (the last to arrive in 1973) were all trading. Led Zeppelin's recording studio had opened nearby, the *Rocky Horror Show* stage production was running each night at Chelsea's Royal Court Theatre and Manolo Blahnik's first shoe shop opened its doors in Old Church Street. Chelsea was now officially a design destination that attracted a young, cool crowd who craved newness and innovation.

The creation of the first collection, *Village* – and its subsequent success – dovetailed with the departure of Robin Guild from both the business and their marriage as he went on to set up a new store – Homeworks – on Pimlico Road later that year. Guild was on her own, with no formal training, very little money and with limited experience. She was, however, armed with a resolute determination, a strong belief in her own instinct, a yearning for independence and a small, devoted team who cared passionately about her and her vision. She would later describe this period to journalist Christina Aziz as: 'years of hard struggle – I was in at the deep end but I knew I had to make it work.'

And make it work, she did. The next few years would see Guild establishing herself as a woman in business – learning through experience, unafraid to ask questions and push boundaries, navigating the various pitfalls of business with differing levels of success.

From top: artwork for the *Geranium* collection, 1976; early mood boards featuring the *Village* collection, 1975; the *Geranium* collection, 1976; a Designers Guild Kids bed, 1998.

A pivotal moment was meeting the renowned knitwear and tapestry artist Kaffe Fassett in 1975. She was struck by his tactile 3D work and his free, flamboyant style. During a visit to his studio, she saw an enormous panel entitled *Geranium* and, in her own words, 'saw a fabric'. Together, they set about creating repeats and a collection that would embody his work, and in 1976 Designers Guild launched the *Geranium* collection of fabrics and wallpapers. It was an instant hit, with both consumers and the interior design trade beating a steady path to the doors of the showroom. Distributors from Belgium, Spain and France (including the soignée ladies of Etamine, Françoise Dorget and Marilyn Gaucher, who were keen to become the French agents for Designers Guild in Paris) were all among the early adopters of Guild's look. Kaffe would go on to design a further three collections for Designers Guild; with each one, the Designers Guild brand became more established.

In 1976, Guild and the team exhibited at the prestigious *Biennale des éditeurs de la Décoration*, held in Paris' old Gare de la Bastille. The exhibition had been the bastion of the major French fabric houses like Pierre Frey, Canovas, Lelièvre, etc., and '*la petite Anglaise*', as she became known in France, was viewed at first with mild bemusement. Then, the likes of Pierre Frey and Manuel Canovas embraced her vision and welcomed her into the fold. The company went on to exhibit in Paris every two years, which in turn would lead to a wider global distribution and the growth of a uniquely international customer base. Today, exports account for well over half the company's sales.

As the brand went on to gain greater recognition, Guild was also intent on pushing herself and the company creatively. Whilst her lack of formal training and experience could sometimes feel like a hindrance, in other ways it liberated her from the constraints of usual practice, and as a young, single woman she used her instincts to gain new ground.

Following on from the success of the artist-inspired collections with Kaffe Fassett, she went on to enlist the services of Lillian Delevoryas – an American watercolourist whose delicate renderings of flowers she loved. Reproducing every nuance of the painter's brushstrokes was key to the success of these collections; *Poppy Vase, Watercolour* and *Tricia Guild Soft Furnishings* owed much to the new printing technique of Galvano machines. The result was a look that would define the late 1970s – romantic, delicate and coordinated (not matching) fabrics, wallpapers and accessories that felt new and different. The look would also come to embody Designers Guild as the likes of *Tea Rose* and *Paper Roses* were sold by the mile throughout the world. With her central, ever present

vision of lifestyle, Guild created cushions and accessories to complement her collections. It led to the publication of her book, *Soft Furnishings*, in which she showed how to create those same accessories at home. It was a huge commercial success and, as another new decade dawned, she and the company had not only survived but were beginning to really thrive.

In order to keep growing (growth being a key part of Guild's mantra), she set up her own studio in the early 1980s at the top of the offices above the showroom at 277 King's Road, where she worked with textile designers to cultivate and create her own artistic language. This didn't necessarily prevent her from working with other artists she loved. Indeed, she went on to produce collections with renowned ceramicist Janice Tchalenko, German abstract artist Michael Heindorff and the mighty titan of modern art, Howard Hodgkin.

In 1985, her reputation was such that another titan – this time of retail – came calling. George Davies had set up the Next chain of fashion stores in 1982 and had transformed the look of the high street with his up-to-the-minute range of clothing for men and women. When he wanted to create a series of homewares, he looked no further than Tricia Guild. Setting up a separate studio for the Next brand, Guild spearheaded the Next Interiors look and in so doing, brought her unique interpretations for home to the high street.

By 1986 – another pivotal year for the company – there were two stores on King's Road: the original fabric and wallpaper showroom; and, three doors down, a unit dedicated to Guild's guiding principle – lifestyle. Here, she showed her own personal take on interiors, always complemented with one-off pieces of art and ceramics (one of her greatest loves) as well as unusual, small runs of accessories that she had painstakingly sourced. She delighted in showing traditional forms of art in new ways – pictures and ceramics in furnished room sets rather than galleries – and the public responded. Agents and distributors from all over the world were keen to stock her collections and the company was now well represented throughout Europe, Australia and the Far East. To capitalise on her new confidence and success, she instinctively knew that the company needed a better structure to move forwards.

Tricia's brother, Simon Jeffreys, had been working as a chartered accountant in corporate finance in Hong Kong for Coopers & Lybrand and was nearing the end of his tenure there, due to return home.

FROM TOP: Tricia Guild and George Davies of Next, 1985; Tricia Guild at home in London, 1998; Tricia Guild and her daughter Lisa, 1995; Tricia Guild in Brazil, 2013.

Jeffreys had an innate sense for business and Guild invited him to join her company. He recognised the potential of the brand and became a partner in the business in 1986, with Tricia as Managing Director. Simon instigated a clear management structure and expanded the number of collections produced each year with a view to taking on the world.

By 1989, they had opened the first Designers Guild office and showroom in Munich. An outpost in Paris followed in 1993, as did one in Milan in 1997. Quickly, they extended and expanded their already strong relationships with the trade throughout Europe, the USA, Australia, New Zealand and the Far East. Sales teams were recruited for export and home markets, and as collections were launched each season and exhibited at major fairs internationally, turnover dramatically increased. The stores on King's Road were also expanded with three further units, creating a Homestore that would become an international destination for the design cognoscenti. From a modest collection of 70 fabrics in 1980 and a turnover of £2 million, the company's fortunes doubled, trebled and more as the new millennium beckoned.

The continued success was due in part to the introduction of more specialised collections – the Designers Guild Kids brand, an instant success in 1989, was one such direction. The Kids brand grew with new collections every two years for over ten years – each collection launched was accompanied by beautiful photography, brochures and marketing campaigns and delivered to a public that clamoured for the latest Designers Guild offering for children's furnishings. The approach wasn't confined to the Kids collections – Guild knew only too well the power of the visual image and, even to this day, takes great care to direct every single marketing campaign for each and every product launch.

Following on closely from the children's ranges and embodying the spirit of Guild's belief in lifestyle, collections of furniture, bedlinen, towels, blankets, throws, cushions, rugs and paint, as well as home fragrance and leather goods followed, with the company establishing a strong licensing division. Each component closed the circle of Guild's unique vision for a receptive and increasingly design-savvy public. Unsurprisingly, the company went on to win the Queen's Award for Export Achievement twice, as well as many international awards throughout the following decades. In 2008, the company was awarded 22nd place in the Sunday Times PwC Profit Track 100, as one of Britain's fastest growing privately owned firms – and Guild was honoured with an OBE from Her Majesty Queen Elizabeth II for services to interior design.

FROM TOP: Tricia Guild receiving the Queen's Award for Export Achievement, 1992; the OBE, 2008; at the launch of The Royal Collection, 2008; with her brother, Simon Jeffreys, 2009.   # 21

As other product categories were introduced, collections of fabrics and wallpapers were similarly significantly expanded. Plains and textures had always been a component of the range but they were further developed in 2002 with the introduction of the Designers Guild Essentials brand. Incorporating hundreds of different plain textures in a multitude of colourways, including masses of neutrals, this new division offered plainer fabrics for a huge variety of end uses and grounded the creativity of the printed and woven work. Capitalising, the company built further on their existing 'contracts' division, substantially increasing their offer of flame-retardant and high-performance fabrics and wallcoverings.

The company continued to break new ground – always surprising their client base with fresh creativity and ingenuity. The expansion of a variety of different interior styles was another major milestone, with the Designers Guild brands division enlisting designers such as Jasper Conran, Emily Todhunter, William Yeoward and Christian Lacroix to create collections which were then developed, produced and distributed under licence by Designers Guild. In 2009, the first range for The Royal Collection of Fabric and Wallpaper (part of The Royal Household) further cemented the company's reputation as a unique destination for all sorts of interior disciplines and styles.

Today, Designers Guild continues to thrive. It operates with the ethos and philosophy that remain rooted in its early years – creativity, ingenuity, innovation and quality, with a contemporary spirit that suffuses the company's every step. Still privately owned and run as a family business, there is a very real sense of unity and vision that runs from the newest and most junior member of staff to those at the top. Many key staff have been with the company for over 25 years and there is a shared vision and sense of teamwork that pervades the atmosphere.

Now available in over 70 markets worldwide and with a turnover well in excess of £50 million a year, the company is ranked as one of the top three most recognised interiors brands across Europe and Tricia Guild's unyielding vision reinforces her standing as one of the great icons of the design industry. From a simple, instinctive fascination with colour and textile, coupled with a thirst for success, she, together with Simon Jeffreys and the team, has built a company that is quite simply a world leader. Guild herself joins the ranks of illustrious women with style (but no training), including Sibyl Colefax, Nancy Lancaster, Syrie Maugham and Elsie de Wolfe, who have changed the way we decorate our homes.

FROM TOP: *Veronese* collection, Spring 2019; interior of the King's Road Homestore, 2019; Tricia Guild in the new paint store, 2018; detail from 'Otto Mosaic' wallpaper, 2019.

The *Indian Summer* exhibition, 1994.

The Designers Guild stand at Maison et Objet, 2005.

The first *Indian Summer* exhibition, 1993.

Exhibition stand, 2009.

The launch of *Pattern*, September 2006.

The cushion wall at the Homestore.

Paris Deco Off, 2018.

Paris Deco Off, 2018.

Tricia Guild, Stockholm, September 2017.

The launch of *Colour Deconstructed*, São Paulo, 2013.

At the V&A for 'A Certain Style', 2014.

The Designers Guild stand at Sleep, 2018.

Interior of the new Paris showroom, September 2016.

As previous.

As previous.

The *Sofienburg* collection, 2011.

Tricia Guild, *Elle Decoration*, 'Best British Brand', October 2010.

From the *Jaipur Rose* collection, Autumn/Winter 2018.

Designers Guild Chicago showroom, 2002.

Giardino Segreto collection, 2018.

The Munich showroom, Autumn/Winter 2019.

In the garden at the Homestore, 2017.

The Stockholm showroom, 2013.

Tricia Guild, Spring 2019.

Preceding pages: the Designers Guild creative studio. This page: Printing the 'Issoria' design from *Jardin des Plantes* collection.

Far from being a remote figurehead of the company she founded, Tricia Guild is actively and passionately involved in every aspect of Designers Guild's creative direction and corporate processes. She is distinctly aware that the company is the embodiment of her vision and, together with the CEO (her brother, Simon Jeffreys), pursues excellence at every step and with every endeavour.

Heading the studio and overseeing the entire creative process – from the design of new products, through to product development, photography, the creation of exhibition stands and marketing campaigns, the design of overseas showrooms and, of course, the design of the flagship stores – is a day-to-day business for Guild. The principle of lifestyle that drove her in the early days remains at the forefront of the company's ventures and shapes the way products are created. Each design starts its life with a seed of an idea or point of inspiration – often 'planted' by Guild herself and always with an artist's brush or pencil. The designers collate ideas and paint and sketch, experiment and trial – working through ideas and themes to create a body of work that Guild steers, guides and ultimately edits into a collection. The creative process can take up to two years from start to finish and at each step, Guild will nudge and nurture – moulding the artwork into styles and looks that will eventually reach the market, creating notable trends. Armed with the edited designs, she works closely with the development team – identifying the best weavers, printers and manufacturers to translate the designs into various products. Since the early days of hand screen printing, the company has employed a variety of techniques and methods to achieve its aims – from rotary Galvano printing to state-of-the-art digital printing. This method enables greater freedom of design and is so true to the original artwork that it has become something of the company's trademark.

Complementing the many textiles and wallpapers are the host of products that fulfil Guild's lifestyle ambition – importantly, accessories are not merely designs derived from their fabric counterparts, but rather created with each specific purpose in mind. The result is broad, multi-layered collections that have real dimension and depth. Paint, furniture, rugs, cushions, bed and bath, as well as stationery and home fragrance – each element conveys its own spirit and further underlines the brand's philosophy, whilst offering accessibility in both design and price point.

The entire composition is brought to life at the company's flagship stores in Chelsea and Marylebone, where the various collections are shown as displays alongside a selection of eclectic and edited pieces. Contemporary furniture by Cappellini, HAY, Knoll and B&B Italia might sit

FROM TOP: hand printing in the early days of the company; Tricia Guild checking initial print runs; fabric being woven, detail; Tricia Guild at the wallpaper printers.

alongside antique or mid-century modern pieces. Carefully sourced pictures and one-off pieces of art – a key element of Guild's style – are shown with an ever-changing selection of goods for the stylish contemporary home. They are all shown in the same way that one might use the products at home – a recreation of a way of life that is the essence of the company's image. The resident interior design team at the stores undertake projects large and small and take pride in translating Guild's creations into a variety of situations. The stores represent the heartbeat of Designers Guild – after all, it is where the story started and it is here that the vision continues to evolve most pertinently.

Guild and Jeffreys meet formally every Monday morning and the week is peppered with meetings of senior management teams who set the agenda, yet are constantly open to feedback and new ideas, setting the tone of a family company that is equally dynamic and professional. Jeffreys was key in organising the structure of the company, reinvigorating processes and initiating new ideas, and the whole team pride themselves on their reputation for innovation and efficiency as well as creativity and exceptional service.

At every step, Guild uses her experience and expertise to full effect – from finalising the initial print runs of each new textile (where she has been known to make last-minute, seemingly minor alterations in her quest for perfection), to planning and designing each photographic campaign that will set the tone of that season's look. Concurrently, the visual merchandising team will be planning the look of each international showroom – considering local tastes and styles while remaining true to the corporate vision, resulting in an international standing that regional teams guard and cultivate. Communications and PR teams work closely with Guild and Jeffreys to manage the image of the brand and the news it dispenses, while every stage of bringing product to market is managed in-house so that a consistent pace is set with Guild and Jeffreys at the helm. Sales and marketing teams are based throughout Europe and worldwide and regularly meet at the company's purpose-built headquarters, discussing feedback, planning sales strategies and constantly building on their relationships with clients and teams alike. Customer service teams, speaking a total of ten different languages, process around 50,000 order lines a month which are fulfilled – within 24 hours of ordering – from the company's state-of-the-art logistics centre in West London. The team take around 2,500 calls a day, with 98 per cent of orders processed and shipped correctly on the first attempt.

FROM TOP: 'strike offs' from the *Pavonia* collection, 2012; in the studio, detail; printing the *Bloomsbury Rose* collection, 2015; cleaning the rollers in the printworks.

Every bit as important as the products at Designers Guild are the staff. Both Guild and Jeffreys are instinctive talent spotters and greatly value and nurture their staff. It is of note that the Designers Guild team are known in the industry for their loyalty and commitment – many have worked at the company for decades and thus there exists an innate understanding and working fluency that, put simply, aids an ease of communication and decision making that is vital for any business. Promotions often – and ideally – come from within the company structure and a sense of career progression is intrinsic to those who work at Designers Guild. Many are multi-lingual – a nod to the company's overseas success – and visitors to the company's West London HQ often remark on a distinctive atmosphere: a dynamic energy mixed with a heads-down, hands-on approach and good-humoured familiarity, which are the order of the day; there is a very real sense of relaxed togetherness and a cohesive ambition.

Jeffreys updates all staff regularly on corporate performance and Guild ensures that all staff attend creative presentations and new launches so that each and every member feels involved and party to a joint vision. Guild was one of the first to recognise the importance of a well-designed staff café, installing one on site from the very beginning. Back in 1990, with the introduction of Café Indigo at their West London HQ, the staff café even made it to the cover of *The World of Interiors* and was genuinely ground breaking in serving staff with fresh, seasonal, healthy food in a beautifully designed, comfortable space.

Staff are encouraged to socialise, and the DG Together programme – the in-house social committee – brings staff from all aspects of the business together in regular activities and charitable fund-raising initiatives.

The brand's intrinsic pursuit of quality has, more recently, taken on a more ecologically friendly approach. Careful recycling, electric delivery vehicles and the minimising of plastics, where possible, are just some of the initiatives in place.

The longevity of the brand owes much to its consistent quest for creativity and innovation and its unwavering belief in these guiding principles.

FROM TOP: Tricia Guild in the design studio; Tricia Guild with the weavers and embroiderers in India; printing Designers Guild *Scenes and Murals*; printing an *Imari* collection fabric.

Tricia Guild Soft Furnishings, gravure printed, 1980.

Village collection hand-printed wallpaper, 1976.

'Fioravanti', flock-printed wallpaper.

Fabrics from *Jaipur Rose* collection, digitally printed.

Imari collection fabrics.

Plain wool tweeds, 2018.

Glazed chintz plains; *Doubleglaze* and *Moonshine*, 1982.

Woven velvets.

Plain pure linen from the *Brera* collection.

Fabrics from the *Sakumari* collection launch on a variety of basecloths, 1995.

Mood board, *Kusumam* campaign shoot, 1993.

Mood board, *Phulkari* campaign shoot, 1994.

Photo shoot prep for *Kusumam*, 1993.

Designers Guild paint, packed full of pigment, 2019.

More tools of the trade.

Tricia Guild and Simon Jeffreys, CEO of Designers Guild.

Checking 'strike offs' at the printer.

Checking colour reproduction.

The *Angles* collection, 1983.

Designers Guild bedlinen, 1993.

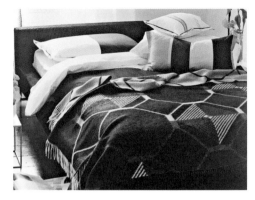

Bedlinen, blankets and cushions, 2010.

Pure linen bedding, 2018.

Biella linen bedding in 12 colours.

Printed percale bedding, Autumn/Winter 2019.

Woven and printed throws and blankets, 2018.

The smooth sofa in *Brera Moda*, 2018.

Printed and woven cushions, Autumn/Winter 2019.

Woven rugs, 2017.

Plains and textures, Autumn/Winter 2017.

Woven geometric rug, Autumn/Winter 2018.

Pure cotton towels in up to 14 colours.

Fabrics, rugs and cushions for the outdoor collection.

Home fragrance, 2009.

Digitally printed linen throw, Spring/Summer 2019.

The 'Balance' sofa, Spring/Summer 2019.

Cushions and textures, Spring/Summer 2018.

King's Road Homestore, 2019.

The 'Wedge' sofa and Designers Guild essentials, 2017.

Vintage furniture in the store, 2018.

Designers Guild paint swatches, 2019.

Furniture and accessories, 2016.

Table linen, 2017.

Preceding pages: left: *Phulkari*, 1994; right: *Jaipur Rose*, 2018. This page: *Kusumam*, 1994.

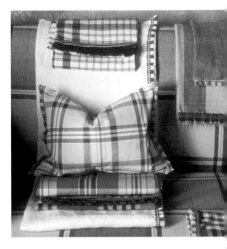

To even the most casual of observers, it is clear that the Designers Guild collections are infused with the influences of the global traveller. Whether it is the deft and confident use of colour or the reimagining of exotic, oriental motifs, there is a sense of other cultures and other lands that sets the brand apart. For a designer born and bred in England, Tricia Guild has always had a distinctly international approach. As a child, her family would travel throughout Europe and later she would take every opportunity to visit other countries and absorb their cultures. She is quoted in her book, *Colour Deconstructed*, as saying: 'People say you are what you eat, but in my opinion – you are what you see.' Her desire to see and her ability to absorb would later influence her tastes and style and thus her work.

India was one of the first places Guild visited and it made a lasting and profound impression: 'I was struck by the energy of the sub-continent – its people, the colours, the rituals and traditions, their dignity and of course the bustling cities and the quiet landscapes.' India with its inherent, instinctive confidence proved to be a major influence on the designer and remains an annual destination to this day. India was also the spark that lit the flame for the first collection, *Village*, and its influence has continued to suffuse Guild's work ever since, both consciously and subliminally.

Contrasting with the exuberance of India, visits to Japan in the 1980s instilled a minimalism and appreciation of form and function that equally appealed to the designer. The Japanese respect for tradition, coupled with its eye to the future, perfectly chimes with her own outlook. Constantly travelling with work through most of Europe – Italy, France, Scandinavia, to name a few – her ever-open eyes would absorb, edit and eventually translate their effects into her work. Ever careful to make the most of every minute in any destination, Guild avidly visits markets, museums and galleries, stores, ateliers and gardens to attain a true sense of each place and discover new ideas.

The result is collections inspired by almost every corner of the globe, while the stores' offerings include edited accessories and pieces sourced on her travels; items that are equally integral to the company's international flavour.

FROM TOP: woven Indian checks, *Kashipur*, 1995; *Sakumari* collection, 1995; wallpapers and borders, *Kalamkari*, 1994; *Jalapuri* silks, 1995.

Few people can claim to have shaped the taste
of a nation, but Tricia Guild is one of them.

Robert Johnstone, 1996

With enviable skill, Tricia Guild knows how to
change direction to capture the mood of the
moment. Now her look is sharpened and more
aggressive, distinctively mixing modern with old.

Nonie Nieswand, *Vogue Living*

Tricia Guild in Sintra, Portugal, on the campaign shoot for Spring/Summer 2015. 　# 43

FROM LEFT: *Karahana* collection, 1996; 'Bandhani', 1994; *Jhati* wallpapers, 1995.

FROM LEFT: *Sakumari* collection, 1995; *Kusumam*, 1993; *Jalapuri* silks, 1993.

LEFT, FROM TOP: *Santa Margherita*, 1993; *Village*, 1976; *Kalamkari*, 1994; RIGHT: detail from *Village*, 1976.

TOP: *Amrapali*, 2011; BOTTOM LEFT; *Sofienburg*, 2011; BOTTOM CENTRE: *Jardin des Plantes*, 2015; BOTTOM RIGHT: *Kasuri* wallpapers, 2012.

FROM TOP: *Kusumam*, 1993; the *Indian Summer* exhibition, 1993; *Jalapuri* silks, 1993.

50 #   A selection of silks, prints and plains from the *Kusumam*, *Jalapuri* and *Tindall* collections, 1993.

CLOCKWISE FROM TOP LEFT: *Mei P'ing*, 1995; *Coromandel*, 2004; *Madame Butterfly*, 2007; *Rajkot* and *Jalaja*, 1997.

LEFT: *Oriental Garden*, 2007; TOP RIGHT: *Jalaja* and *Rajkot*, 1997; BOTTOM RIGHT: *Oriental Garden*, 2007.   # 55

LEFT: *Foscari* silks, 2005; TOP RIGHT: *Brocatelle* weaves, *Foscari* silks, 2005; BOTTOM RIGHT: *Caprifoglio*, 2014.

Samarkand, Foscari, 2005.

TOP: *Bukhara* flock prints, 2005; BOTTOM LEFT: *Samarkand*, 2005; BOTTOM CENTRE: *Foscari*, 2005; BOTTOM RIGHT: *Bukhara*, 2005.   # 59

A traveller in the true sense, she gleans inspiration

everywhere: from the arts and opera to the

fragment of an Indian Sari or an Italian Fresco.

Rosemarie Hillier, *House & Garden*, 2001

Linnaeus wallpapers , 2011.

Scenes and Murals, 2019.

ALL IMAGES: prints and wallpapers, *Shanghai Garden* collection, 2015.

ALL IMAGES: *Shanghai Garden* collection, 2015.

Scenes and Murals, 2019.

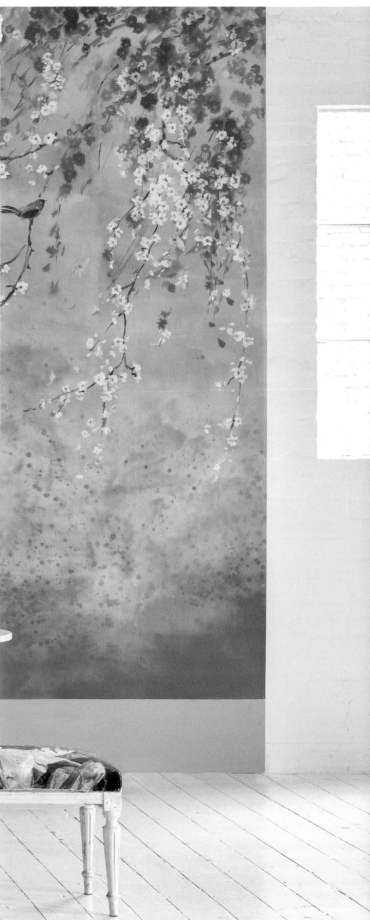

PRECEDING PAGES: LEFT: *Florimund*, 2008; RIGHT: *Le Poème de Fleurs*, 2019. THIS PAGE: *Grandiflora*, 1987.

In the same way that a fabric is made up of different threads and an artist's canvas of many colours and textures, it would be fair to say that the work of Tricia Guild is composed of various elements and inspirations that come together in unique and distinctive collections.

One of the most consistent threads of her vocabulary has been her use of flowers, the landscape and nature in her designs. An ardent gardener and lifelong lover of flowers, Guild's approach to interpreting their beauty is intrinsic to the company's work.

In some of the early designs from the 1970s, such as *Paper Roses* and *Geranium*, the painterly, watercolour brushstrokes of flowers, leaves and petals felt fresh and new and were in direct contrast to the more formal styles of floral fabrics and papers that existed at that time. The subtle variations of tone and shade employed by the artist captured the natural beauty of each petal and with the onset of Galvano printing, the hand-painted artwork could be reproduced as faithfully as it was possible to do. This natural depiction of flowers, plants and trees would evolve over the decades, becoming a hallmark of the company's style that grew richer and stronger in colour and texture in the 1980s with the voluptuous blooms of *Grandiflora* and *Spring Classics,* and throughout the 1990s with more contemporary modern studies of flowers in a palette of clear, fresh tones.

As a new millennium dawned, the flowered fabrics by Designers Guild became more classical in inspiration but electrifyingly modern at the same time. The dramatic blooms of *Cristobal, Inessa* and *China Rose* reinvented flowers in yet another new spirit, while the advent of digital printing allowed Guild the freedom to create on a larger scale. The modern-day classics of *Mariedal, Sofienburg* and *Zepherine and Peonia Grande* continued to push boundaries and were used alongside checks and stripes and cut velvets for contemporary glamour.

Flowers in their natural state have also played their part in Guild's career. Having written three books on the lyrical beauty of flowers and plants, her style of collecting simple stems and leaves together in spare, structural forms has also become something of a trademark and again went against the tide of complex bouquets and arrangements.

The landscape and nature in its purest form continue to inspire the designer and her work today and are fundamental to the spirit of Designers Guild.

FROM TOP: *Tapisserie*, 1988; *Oriental Flowers* by Kaffe Fassett, 1989; *Chintz Classics*, 1985; *Cherry Orchard*, 2005.   # 75

The way she approached the rocks, trees, water and flowers,
very slowly and as if she were studying them – I'd never seen
anything like it before. The interplay of the colours and light
fascinated her. She was extraordinarily in tune with her environment.

Jeppe Wikström on Tricia Guild, 1999

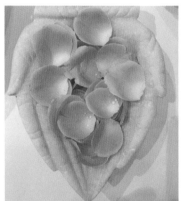

There are few things as naturally beautiful as a
handful of fresh flowers from the garden, simply
arranged with a single leaf to lift one's soul.

Tricia Guild

TOP LEFT: *Grandiflora*, 1988; TOP CENTRE: *Sarafan*, 2006; TOP RIGHT: *Spring Flower*, 1986; BOTTOM: *Florimund*, 2008.

CLOCKWISE FROM TOP LEFT: *Arabella*, 2008; *Florimund*, 2008; *Whitewell*, 2009; *Florimund*, 2008.

FROM TOP: *Pavilion*, 2010; *Pavilion*, 2010; *Zephirine*, 2010.

Zephirine collection, 2010.

LEFT, FROM TOP: *Amrapali*, 2011; decorative flowers; *Madhuri*, 2014; RIGHT: *Madhuri*, 2014.

Seraphina collection, 2013.

Majolica collection, 2017.

Shanghai Garden collection, 2015.

ALL IMAGES: *Caprifoglio* collection, 2015.

Caprifoglio collection, 2015.

ALL IMAGES: *Caprifoglio* collection, 2015.

ALL IMAGES: details of flowers, 2018.

As in a three-dimensional collage, Tricia combines colour

and light, patterns and fabrics with furnishing elements

and the floral world. The result is the definition of a very

unique way of interpreting the contemporary lifestyle.

Livia Peraldo Matton, Editor of *Elle Décor Italia*, 2019

Jardin des Plantes collection, 2016.

ALL IMAGES: *Tulipa Stellata*, 2017.

FROM TOP: *Veronese*, 2019; *Jaipur Rose*, 2018; *Jaipur Rose*, 2018.

Jaipur Rose collection, 2018.

TOP LEFT: *Jaipur Rose*, 2018; BOTTOM LEFT: *Le Poème de Fleurs*, 2019; RIGHT: *Jaipur Rose*, 2018.   # 111

FROM TOP: *Veronese*, 2019; flower detail; *Le Poème de Fleurs*, 2019.

PRECEDING PAGES: LEFT: *Le Poème de Fleurs*, 2019; RIGHT: *Brera* collection plains, 2009. THIS PAGE: Tricia Guild's London home, 1995.

From the beginning, Tricia Guild has carved her own path and, more often than not, it has led her work in an entirely different direction to the prevailing style and looks of the time. In the 1970s, while rust-coloured Dralon® and orange velvet drapes were the look of the moment in the fashionable sitting rooms of the land, Guild's first collection, *Village*, introduced the world to her interpretation of Indian block prints – simple, clear designs in a palette of hues from soft pastel to vibrant and dynamic on white grounds. The scale, too, varied and Guild mixed colours, tones and textures in her shop with an inherent ease, creating a complete look that immediately felt fresh, new and *daring*. Her indomitable spirit has infused every collection since and there must be more than just a touch of the elegant rebel within her psyche, for her work has continued to surprise and astonish throughout the life of the brand.

In the 1980s, her bold spirit took the company in another new direction that would become synonymous with the sense of daring for which the company is known. Richly printed fabrics and wallpapers captured the spirit of India and the East in the *Kusuman, Sakumari, Phulkari, Karahana* and *Ashrafi* collections – with unexpected colour combinations including singing cobalt blue, sunshine yellow and lime. Vivid fuchsia, saffron and magenta were employed with bold, artistic brushstrokes and an intensity that was direct and oozed confidence yet, thanks to clever marketing campaigns, showed the consumer how to use them in their own home, inspiring them to live with the new rather than interpretations from the past.

As the decades progressed, collections took on a more classical spirit as Guild reinvented the formal textiles of the seventeenth and eighteenth centuries. Brocades and cut velvets, printed silks and embroidered organzas, flocked and embellished wallpapers – all were reimagined in bold scales and exciting shades that were considered brave yet also suited to more conventional spaces due to their inherently traditional roots. As well as patterns, bold mixes of plain colour inspired consumers in their masses to be brave and to live with colours in a way that had hitherto been used only by the few. Using every component of a living space – from furniture, curtains and walls to bedlinen, throws and cushions – the look was accessible to everyone who was inspired by her work.

Challenging the style edicts of the time rather than intentionally defying them is a cornerstone of Guild's modus operandi, questioning whether something can be improved, refined or contempororised. Her sights consistently set to the future, she remains a step ahead of the zeitgeist.

FROM TOP: *Village* wallpapers, 1976; *Damas Fleuri*, 1988; *Arietta* taffetas, 2011; *Varese*, 2004. # 117

There is nothing beige about Designers Guild. Tricia Guild's vibrant sense of colour and painterly design language makes Designers Guild instantly recognisable, as well as creating the DNA of what has been a strong and consistent brand in a very competitive and demanding industry.

Ilse Crawford

Tricia's amazing sense of color and desire to share it with the world has been an inspiration to me since we met close to 30 years ago.

John Derian, 2009

From left: *Borghese*, 1996; Tricia Guild's London home, 1996; favourite ceramics.

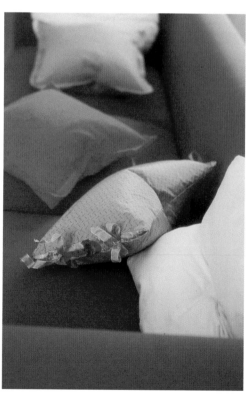

From left: 'Maroushka Metz' chair in *Brera*; *Brera*, 1996; *Fiesole*, 2000.

TOP LEFT: *Brera, Borghese*, 1996; TOP CENTRE: *Brera*, 2006; TOP RIGHT: 'Festival' chairs, 2008; BOTTOM: *Manhattan*, 2009.

Coromandel wallpapers, 2006.   # 123

Arabella flock wallcoverings, 2008.

TOP LEFT: *Coromandel*, 2006; BOTTOM LEFT: *Arabella* wallcoverings, 2008; RIGHT: *Arabella* fabrics and wallcoverings, 2008.   # 125

CLOCKWISE FROM TOP LEFT: *Brera Lino*, *Brera Alta*, 2010; *Manhattan*, 2009; *Fiesole*, 2000; *Quarenghi*, 2007.

FROM TOP: *Manhattan*, 2009; *Manhattan*, 2009; *Barcelona*, 2010.

Zephirine collection, 2010.

ALL IMAGES LEFT: *Brera Alta, Brera Lino*, 2010.

ALL IMAGES: fabrics from 2008 to 2010.

Tricia Guild has been a revolutionary. She has made us brave. The days

of sticking to stale and safe colour schemes have given way to the colour

phenomenon. Increasingly, people now opt for chrome yellow instead

of dirty cream, brilliant blue instead of bland buff and even pillar box red

for their homes. This change in attitude is due, in part, to Tricia Guild,

one of the leading lights in the world of interior decoration in recent years.

Sophie Benge, 'Palette on Parade', *Home Journal* (Hong Kong), 1994

CLOCKWISE FROM TOP LEFT: *Pavonia*, 2012; *Indupala*, 2014; *Varese*, 2017; *Arietta*, 2011.

Majolica collection, 2017.

TOP LEFT: *Amrapali*, 2011; TOP CENTRE: *Sofienburg*, 2011; TOP RIGHT: *Amrapali*, 2011; BOTTOM: *Amrapali*, 2011.

FROM TOP: *Astrakhan*, 2013; *Cheviot*, 2011; *Sukumala*, 2014.

Astrakhan collection, 2013.   # 145

ALL IMAGES: *Chandigarh* collection, 2018.

PRECEDING PAGES: LEFT: *Saraille*, 2012; RIGHT: *Mandora*, 2018. THIS PAGE: *Grandiflora Rose*, 2020.

Artists and designers are often associated with a particular signature, a type of handwriting or look that comes to define their work and thus encapsulate a style – a soundbite that enables consumers to recognise them and, in an instant, feel familiar with their creations. However, Tricia Guild has never been comfortable with being compartmentalised; whichever category she has been assigned, she has consistently proved its boundaries to be too restrictive and, indeed, inaccurate. Designers Guild is known for colour – sometimes strong, vivid colour – yet that is only part of the story.

From the beginning, her work has included plains and neutrals, and softer shades and textures, contradicting the notion that Designers Guild is always richly coloured, floral or patterned. In fact, the success of those intricate, painterly designs and strong colours relies on expanses of plains, whites and neutrals. As such, the library of plains comprises almost half the company's range of fabrics and wallpapers. Similarly, its selection of neutrals and monochromes is vast and offers the dynamism and complexity of designs and textures in soft, easy shades.

Of course, texture becomes ever more important when using plain colour and these are plentiful. From the chintzes and dobby weaves of *Moonshine*, *Doubleglaze*, *Rough Diamond* and *Marquetry* in the 1970s and '80s, the collections have grown substantially to include, among many others, faux suede, assorted weights of linen, velvet, chenille, silk, wool and tweed as well as practical textures designed to meet the rigours of modern life.

The graphic quality of monochrome has always held a particular fascination for Guild. It is a combination that seemingly she never tires of, whether it is used as a single palette over different designs and textures in one space or as a way of adding definition and a graphic modernity to a more classical design.

In 1999, in her book *White Hot*, Guild explained the significant shift. She wrote: 'The balance has changed. I always used more white and natural colours than people may have supposed, but whereas white was previously a "silent partner", it has now moved to centre stage.'

More recently, plains too have been reimagined with the advent of ombrés – shaded washes of colour on wallpapers and fabrics. The *Saraille*, *Padua*, *Capisoli* and *Eberson* collections introduced on a variety of textures from floaty linen to wool and velvet offer tonal gradations of colour that fade to white and natural, adding interest and more than a hint of an artist's watercolour wash.

I can't think of a single room that doesn't benefit from
a dash of white. It acts as a breathing space allowing
other colours and patterns to shine whilst adding
timeless elegance and modernity in equal measure.

Tricia Guild, 2016

So much of the focus of Tricia's and Designers Guild's work is on colour
and pattern, some might find it surprising that she's also a genius
when it comes to working with neutral shades and fabrics. She knows
exactly how to combine different textures to the best possible effect.

Ben Spriggs, Editor, *ELLE Decoration* UK, 2019

156 #   TOP: *Florimund*, 2008; BOTTOM LEFT: *Mei P'ing*, 1995; BOTTOM CENTRE: *Natural Classics*, 1984; BOTTOM RIGHT: *Mahé*, 1993.

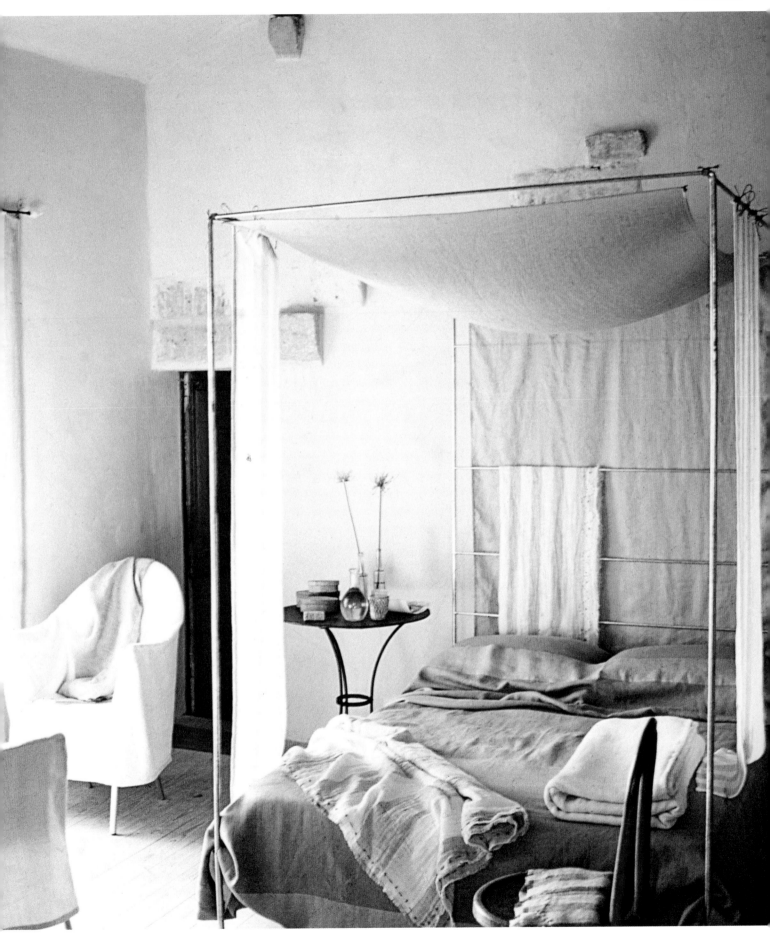

Amalienborg, 2007.

TOP LEFT: *Linnaeus*, 2011; TOP RIGHT: *Quarenghi*, 2011; BOTTOM: *Quarenghi*, 2011. # 159

TOP: Essentials, 2008; BOTTOM LEFT: Essentials, 2009; BOTTOM RIGHT: *Fitzrovia*, 2019.

Pavonia collection, 2012.

TOP LEFT: *Pavonia*, 2012; TOP RIGHT: *Pavonia*, 2012; BOTTOM: *Sukumala*, 2014. # 163

TOP: *Savine*, 2013; BOTTOM: *Saraille*, 2012.

TOP: *Seraphina*, 2013; BOTTOM LEFT: *Couture Rose*, 2016; BOTTOM RIGHT: *Seraphina*, 2013.

Savine collection, 2013.

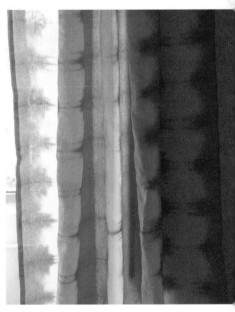

Tricia has an innate sensitivity for colours and decorations

that she mixes and matches with an absolute naturalness.

The shades are always magical and surprising.

Giulio Cappellini

174 # From top: *Shanghai Garden*, 2015; *Couture Rose*, 2016; *Shanghai Garden*, 2015.

TOP LEFT: *Marquisette* silks, 2016; TOP RIGHT: *Sleek* sofa, 2018; BOTTOM: *Palermo* sofas, 2018.   # 177

FROM TOP: *Brera moda* 218; *Marquisette* 2016; *Brera*, 2017.

'Emerald' paint and *Savoie* fabric in Tricia Guild's London home, 2019.

Clockwise from top left: *Padua*, 2013; *Padua*, 2013; *Saraille*, 2012; *Saraille*, 2012.

CLOCKWISE FROM TOP LEFT: *Savoie*, 2018; *Saraille*, 2012; *Savoie*, 2018; *Foscari Fresco*, 2018.   # 181

Foscari Fresco collection, 2018.

LEFT: *Savoie*, 2018; TOP RIGHT: *Palme Botanique*, 2019; CENTRE RIGHT: *Lauziere*, 2018; BOTTOM RIGHT: *Casablanca*, 2017. # 183

TOP LEFT: *Scenes and Murals*, 2019; TOP CENTRE: *Foscari Fresco*, 2019; TOP RIGHT: *Foscari Fresco*, 2019; BOTTOM: *Foscari Fresco*, 2019.

Preceding pages: left: *Pavilion*, 2010; right: *Scenes and Murals*, 2019. This page: *Colonnade*, 2016.

Although nature has played a large part in the creativity behind Designers Guild, it would be inaccurate to assume that flowers have been the sole means of artistic expression. With a constant eye on modernity, structure and architectural detail, another element of the brand's success has been the geometric stripes, checks and intricately detailed graphic designs that have been used on their own and alongside floral fabrics and papers to create an entirely different spirit.

From the earliest collection of block prints inspired by India's architecture in *Village*, and the ground-breaking collection of *Angles* in the 1970s, geometric designs had firmly taken root in the company's style. Although it was lauded by *Vogue* and the press in general, the *Angles* collection was not an immediate commercial success, yet, undaunted, Guild continued to instinctively explore this medium of abstract expression.

Inspired by the paintings of Mark Rothko, Howard Hodgkin and others, this language appealed to her sense of modernity and she would go on to combine the structure of stripes with the expansive freedom of flowers to create a balance in both fabrics and wallpapers that would also become a hallmark. In the 1980s, vivid, vibrant checks and stripes in clashing combinations were woven in shimmering silk and velvet or wool stripes, whilst in the '90s the fascination with architectural details from classical periods would be reimagined in a palette of colours that spanned the spectrum.

Latterly, the forms of classical ikats, Florentine marbling and even tie-dyed fabrics would explore a softer incarnation of the geometric, roundly defying the notion that her look was overtly feminine and floral. Used for wallpapers and a variety of textiles, and employed in interiors alongside plain textures or walls, they depicted a look that was every bit as confident and of the moment; in the process, she appealed to a totally different set of followers. Guild long disputed the idea that a truly modern interior should be devoid of pattern and must rely solely on architectural form and function to be considered progressive. Rather, she showed contemporary interiors that were sleek and elegant, strong and structural, and largely with an absence of expansive flowers to illustrate her own inimitable approach.

Tricia's style is instantly recognisable yet entirely her own –
brave in both colour and pattern. That Designers Guild has been
in business for 50 years and still feels current and covetable
is testament to her huge dedication and distinctive eye.

Hatta Byng, Editor of *House & Garden*, 2019

Tricia enables a theatre of colour and pattern
that lights up so many of today's interiors.

Kaffe Fasset, 2019

194 #   TOP: *Oriental Garden*, 2007; BOTTOM LEFT: *Pavilion*, 2010; BOTTOM CENTRE: *Trevelyan*, 2010; BOTTOM RIGHT: *Pavilion*, 2010.

TOP: *Monteverdi*, 2008; BOTTOM: *Quarenghi*, 2007.   # 197

198 #   TOP LEFT: *Quarenghi*, 2007; CENTRE LEFT: *Pavilion*, 2010; BOTTOM LEFT: *Amalienborg*, 2007; RIGHT: *Oriental Garden*, 2007.

All images: *Pavilion* collection, 2010.

Whitewell, 2009.

TOP LEFT: *Pavilion*, 2010; TOP CENTRE: *Majella*, 2016; TOP RIGHT: *Caprifoglio*, 2015; BOTTOM: *Amrapali*, 2011.   # 203

Savine collection, 2013.

FROM TOP: *Pugin*, 2015; *Pugin*, 2015; *Amlapura*; 2014.

208 # CLOCKWISE FROM TOP LEFT: *Majolica*, 2017; *Jardin des Plantes*, 2016; *Majolica*, 2017; *Zardozi*, 2018.

FROM TOP: rugs, 2018; *Fitzrovia*, 2019; *Casablanca*, 2017.

Every time Tricia Guild embraces fresh new colours,

drawing rooms up and down the country take note.

Her ground breaking colour sense may shape trends,

but Tricia Guild still does modern with a soft edge.

Judith Wilson, *House & Garden*, 2000

Mandora collection, 2018.

TOP: *Zardozi*, 2018; BOTTOM LEFT: *Zardozi*, 2018; BOTTOM CENTRE: *Jaipur Rose*, 2018; BOTTOM RIGHT: *Chandigarh*, 2018.   # 215

216 # CLOCKWISE FROM TOP LEFT: *Murrine*, 2017; *Zardozi*, 2018; *Fitzrovia*, 2019; *Chandigarh*, 2018.

Le Poème de Fleurs, 2019.

TOP: *Scenes and Murals*, 2019; BOTTOM: *Fitzrovia*, 2019. # 219

PRECEDING PAGES: Howard Hodgkin collection, 2012. THIS PAGE: Kaffe Fassett's Pots, 1994.

From the earliest days of her company, Tricia Guild felt a natural affinity with the freedom expressed by artists. With no formal training, her approach to fabrics and wallpapers was instinctive and not restricted to designing in pattern repeats. Hers was a creativity that was free and sensitive, perhaps even naïve – always questioning why and why not in her quest for artistic freedom.

When Tricia asked me to design for her next collection back in the late '80s, I'd never done a print in repeat. With her enthusiastic guidance and encouragement, I produced my first artwork for a fabric print. Her passion and appreciation for my work were the ingredients that made our first collaborations so successful. To see the almost unnoticed corner of one of my paintings transformed into yardage was sheer magic that gave me the courage to become the designer and producer I am now. Tricia enables a theatre of colour and pattern that lights up so many of today's interiors.

Kaffe Fassett, July 2019

I am not a fabric designer but I've always been fascinated by the dangerous interaction of textiles and art. In 1986, I seized the opportunity when Tricia Guild asked me to work on fabrics for Designers Guild.

Howard Hodgkin, September 2011

FROM TOP: Tricia and Lisa Guild with Kaffe Fassett, 1979; Howard Hodgkin poster for the International Contemporary Art Fair, 1986; Howard Hodgkin in his studio, 2012.   # 223

Kaffe Fassett b.1937

In the early 1970s, Guild met Kaffe Fassett at one of his exhibitions. Known for designing knitwear (he had already designed collections for Bill Gibb and Missoni), he elevated the seemingly old-fashioned media of needlepoint and tapestry into a uniquely modern art form. This wonderfully free expression struck a chord with Guild: 'I saw possibilities for fabrics in his work – details that would make beautiful wallpapers and repeats.' The result was an artistic partnership that would last for decades. The first collection, *Geranium*, was followed the next year by *Bean and Daisy*, which was a great success, and again in the 1980s and '90s with *Oriental Flowers* and *The Melon Patch*. In each collection, Kaffe's distinctive needlepoint textures were marvellously apparent and gave each textile and paper a unique handwriting.

TOP: 'Poppy' base by Kaffe Fassett, 1977; BOTTOM LEFT: *Bean* and *Daisy* collections, 1978; BOTTOM RIGHT: *Natural Classics*, 1984.

Lillian Delevoryas 1932–2018

Lillian was an American painter-turned-textile artist who came to the UK in 1970 at the suggestion of Kaffe Fassett and Judy Brittain of *Vogue*. Lillian adored the English countryside, and was greatly inspired, in particular, by English country gardens, with their profusions of colour. Her watercolours of flowers had a sensitivity that summed up the mood of the time, and when Guild and Delevoryas met, there was an instant mutual respect and admiration. She created two main collections for Designers Guild – *Poppy Vase* and *Watercolour* – both based on her detailed studies of flowers. Thanks to the use of Galvano printing, which allowed every subtlety and nuance of the artist's brushstrokes to be faithfully reproduced, the resulting fabrics and wallpapers captured the uniqueness of her freedom of expression and were hugely successful. Most notable was *Paper Roses* – an all-over floral in soft, subtle pastel tones that came to define the look of the era and was considered a classic Designers Guild print for many years.

Janice Tchalenko 1942–2018

Janice Tchalenko trained as a ceramicist and potter in the late 1960s and for ten years produced hand-thrown tableware in the Leach tradition. Latterly, she introduced different shapes and bright colours to set a whole new agenda for the studio pottery movement. Guild had admired and collected Tchalenko's work over the years and was keen to translate the glazes and washes of rich, deep colour into fabrics and wallpapers. Guild's ability to spot a style and a look led to an exciting collaboration – the result was a collection called *Waterleaf*, which initiated a richer, darker look for the company. Perfectly capturing the textures and glazes of Janice's ceramics, the work had a more masculine identity than the work of Derevoryas, and Guild mixed the patterns in varying scales with a deftness of touch that became ubiquitous.

TOP: *Watercolour*, 1979; BOTTOM: *Waterleaf*, 1986.　# 225

Michael Heindorff b.1949

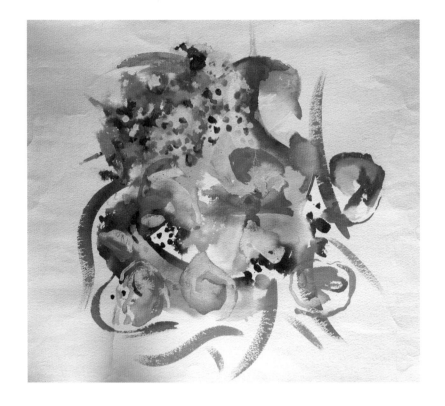

Heindorff is a German painter and print maker who studied – and later taught – at The Royal College of Art. Guild discovered his work in the early 1990s, at an exhibition at the Bernard Jacobson Gallery. A mix of figurative and abstract styles, Heindorff's interpretation of the natural world resulted in a collection of contemporary fabrics for Designers Guild called *Still Life*. Translating the artist's work into a mix of modern fabrics, Guild's emotive response to art was evident as she re-coloured designs into colourways and selected the best base cloths for each design.

Bill Jacklin b.1943

Bill Jacklin studied graphic design in the early 1960s before working at Studio Seven in London. He found the world of graphics rather restrictive and returned to study painting at Walthamstow School of Art and subsequently The Royal College of Art, where he later taught. Known equally for his romantic, yet dramatic pictures, as well as the graphic quality of his prints, Jacklin met Guild in the 1970s . She was immediately struck by the intensity of his work, within which she once again saw fabrics and repeats. The *Anemone* collection was a fine balance of dramatic florals and graphic modernity – a contrast of romance and strength that worked beautifully within an interior.

Howard Hodgkin 1932-2017

Howard Hodgkin, one of the foremost British artists of the last century, was renowned for his masterful use of colour. His paintings were primarily grounded on a remembered experience or emotion – a starting point from which Hodgkin would work over a long period of time to produce layered, richly coloured, sweeping compositions, often extending onto the picture frame. His work had an arresting and extraordinary ability to provoke an emotional response in the viewer, and meeting Hodgkin in the mid 1980s was a seminal moment for Tricia Guild. His passion for India and his love of Matisse, his fearless use of colour and texture and his deeply sensitive approach to each piece of work chimed with her own sensibilities and she was greatly affected by knowing him. When Guild asked Hodgkin to design a collection in 1986, the result was a series of fabrics that captured his broad sensuous brushstrokes and vivid colours in textile form. They proved an instant hit, and were later relaunched in 2012.

TOP: The original 'Large Flower', 1986; BOTTOM LEFT: *Large Leaf*, 2012; BOTTOM RIGHT: *Brushstroke*, 2012.   # 227

PRECEDING PAGES FROM LEFT: John Derian, Christian Lacroix, Ralph Lauren fabrics, The Royal Collection, William Yeoward. THIS PAGE: *Histoires Naturelles* by Christian Lacroix, 2018.

Collaboration has always come easily to Tricia Guild. Since the early days of working with Kaffe Fassett and other artists, she has thrived in partnership with other creative minds. Although single-minded in following her own intuitive expression, she admires and appreciates different interior aesthetics and respects designers and brands who follow a different path and who do so at a similarly high level.

By 1989, Designers Guild had built up an enviable worldwide network of agents and distributors, as well as interior designers, architects and retailers serviced by a team of brilliant salespeople and managers. It made perfect sense to reciprocate the service and to distribute some of the finest names in European design within the UK. Brands such as Etro, Etamine, Bevilacqua and Blue Home, amongst others, joined the ranks whose fabrics and wallpapers were distributed by Designers Guild. With its own small showroom in Chelsea's Old Church Street, the Designers Guild Distribution sub-brand offered a variety of different styles to both trade customers and retail consumers, bringing the best international fabrics to British shores – all serviced seamlessly by the Designers Guild operation.

Following this success, in 1999 Designers Guild became the distributor of Ralph Lauren fabrics and wallpapers throughout Europe and the Middle East. In order to accommodate this prestigious brand, the Designers Guild Distribution division now focused solely on Ralph Lauren.

In subsequent years, the company has invited designers from different fields to design interior fabrics and wallpapers exclusively for the Designers Guild brand. Since 1997, Jasper Conran, Emily Todhunter, Christian Lacroix and The Royal Collection of Fabrics and Wallpapers have all designed collections under their name which Designers Guild have then developed, manufactured and distributed under licence.

Working with the different designers and creative directors, and using her expertise and creative knowledge, Guild has set about interpreting their expressions to create collections that offer even more choice to the consumer but are every bit as independent as the Designers Guild brand itself. Not just confined to fabrics and wallpapers, these endeavours have also taken the form of licensing collaborations, such as a collection of mosaic tile designs by Bisazza and a small collection of rugs for Moooi, as well as a collection of furniture by renowned designer Giulio Cappellini that uses Designers Guild fabrics.

FROM TOP: John Derian NYC, 2018; Isabelle de Borchgrave, 1990; The Royal Collection of Fabrics and Wallcoverings, 2008.   # 231

John Derian

John Derian – a creative maverick who was simply enthralled by the printed images of the past – set up his company in 1989. Scouring flea markets and antique fairs, he would breathe new life into these images through decoupage, an art form for which he has become justly famous. Over the years, the brand has grown to include a variety of different products – postcards and stationery, tote bags and a successful collaboration with Astier de Villatte have all cemented his reputation as a formidable creative force. Tricia Guild sought out his products almost from the beginning and has been selling his work in the King's Road stores since he first started his collection. In 2018, they collaborated on the first collection of John Derian fabrics, with the second launching the following year to a rapturous response.

TOP: *Picture Book*, 2018; BOTTOM LEFT: *Picture Book II*, 2019; BOTTOM CENTRE: *Picture Book*, 2018; BOTTOM RIGHT: *Picture Book II*, 2019.

Histoires Naturelles, 2018.

Christian Lacroix Maison

Having built up a reputation for producing and distributing collections by other brands, Designers Guild were approached by global fashion designer and creative extraordinaire Christian Lacroix. His standing as a designer of haute couture was unrivalled and he was keen to explore other avenues for his talents. The wheels were set in motion for a licensing agreement to produce fabrics, wallpapers and home fashion accessories that would commence in 2011. However, halfway through the process, Christian Lacroix lost control of his own business and his brand, so the task to complete the project fell to his second in command, Sacha Walckhoff. Sacha had worked with Lacroix for many years and knew intimately the essence of the brand. Flamboyant and vibrant, with more than a hint of the eccentric, the Lacroix collections caused a stir in the world of interior design and the partnership continues today with great success.

TOP: *Paradis Barbares*, 2019; BOTTOM FROM LEFT, ALL: *Histoires Naturelles*, 2018.   # 235

Ralph Lauren Home

From the romantic florals of the English countryside to the trading blankets of the American west, Ralph Lauren fabric and wallcovering captures the iconic sensibilities, distinctive vision and unwavering commitment to craftsmanship that have defined the Ralph Lauren Home collection for over thirty years. In Designers Guild, Ralph Lauren recognised a likeminded partner, similarly committed to the highest standards of quality, design and innovation, and in 1999 Designers Guild became the exclusive distributor of Ralph Lauren fabric and wallcovering throughout Europe.

TOP: *Mulholland Drive*, 2018; BOTTOM LEFT: *Black Palms*, 2017; BOTTOM CENTRE: *Islesboro*, 2019; BOTTOM RIGHT: *Islesboro*, 2019.

Buckingham, 2015.

The Royal Collection

In 2007, Designers Guild were approached by The Royal Collection Trust – a division of the Royal Household that cares for the palaces and possessions of the sovereign that are held in state for the nation by HM Queen Elizabeth II. The concept was to design, develop and produce a collection of fabrics, wallpapers and accessories directly inspired by the contents of The Royal Collection. It was an enormous achievement to be the only brand granted exclusive access to the royal palaces, including Buckingham Palace and Windsor Castle, as well as the exquisite collections of art and objets within. Employing an entirely different aesthetic, Guild created ranges inspired by The Royal Collection that were a world away from her own work at Designers Guild. Richly embroidered and embellished, the collections would draw on tradition and stately elegance to offer the consumer a new interpretation of regal glamour. The collections were a great success in the UK, the USA and elsewhere.

TOP: *Buckingham*, 2015; BOTTOM LEFT: *St James's*, 2014; BOTTOM CENTRE: *Savigny*, 2009; BOTTOM RIGHT: *Connaught*, 2017.

William Yeoward

William Yeoward started his creative life at Designers Guild, working closely with Tricia Guild in the late 1970s. Having left the company after some seven years, he set up his own practice as an interior designer, creating homes for the elite of British society, including the then prime minister Margaret Thatcher. He also began working with renowned crystal maker, Timothy Jenkins, to create his own interpretation of eighteenth and nineteenth-century crystal pieces, and added to his collection of goods with handmade furniture and lighting. He was a name to watch, developing his style with a modern British aesthetic that converted perfectly to fabrics, wallpapers and accessories. The William Yeoward collections offered classic with a twist of elegance in a palette that is adored by many, both in the UK and in overseas territories.

TOP: *Alberesque*, 2014; BOTTOM LEFT: *Florian*, 2019; BOTTOM CENTRE: *Florian*, 2019; BOTTOM RIGHT: *Astasia*, 2013.

THE PHILOSOPHY

ARTISTRY, CREATIVITY, INNOVATION AND QUALITY
ARE AT THE HEART OF WHAT WE DO

TRICIA GUILD PAINT BOX
TRICIA GUILD PAINT BOX
TRICIA GUILD PAINT BOX

PRECEDING PAGES: Tricia Guild with a selection of books and magazines, 2019. THIS PAGE: Tricia Guild at the V&A, London, 2017.

From the earliest moments of her career, Tricia Guild was intuitively aware that for her vision to be successful, people needed to see her work in a manner that they could relate to. The concept of lifestyle, as we have learned, was always at the very heart of her work. From that first display of the *Village* collection at 277 King's Road, she has been emboldened by the response that showing her work in this way has engendered.

Since that time, she has consistently and actively promoted a visual image, a point of view and a unique perspective. Whether it be displays in the flagship stores and showrooms, photography and marketing campaigns, press and publicity through countless media, or any one of her 18 books, she has instinctively brought the vision from her own imagination to life.

Guild's books have fostered a loyal following and within them she has explored her own inspirations, nature, architecture, flowers and, of course, the use of colour and pattern in the world of design and decoration. Through them and through the hundreds of visual images she has created, one can see the evolution of the designer's imagination and artistry.

The result is a dynamic propagation of the Designers Guild brand and what it stands for – inspiring so many along the way, whilst also allowing for the more personal pursuit of her own creativity.

FROM TOP: at a book signing, 2009; lecturing in Russia, 2017; signing copies of *In My View*, 2019.   # 245

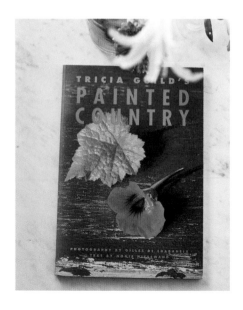

246 #   Tricia Guild has written 19 books to date, several of which have been published in translation.

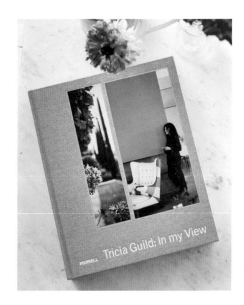

Looking Forward

The celebration of a career milestone brings the chance to reflect; an opportunity to consider the achievements, the highs and the lows, of a lifetime's work. For Tricia Guild, looking back does not come easily. More often than not, she is finely tuned to face forward; to look ahead to a new world of possibilities. As each new collection or exhibition approaches, her creative energy is firmly focused on the works in progress.

In this instance, on the fiftieth anniversary of Designers Guild, she is immersed in the Spring/Summer 2020 collection – *Grandiflora Rose*, which celebrates the beauty of an English country garden but does so, as usual, with a twist that is uniquely Guild. Intricately drawn magnolia blossoms are coloured in unusual, soft-neutral tones, but their expansive, extraordinary scale announces a new contemporary spirit. A vivacious all-over floral, *Grandiflora Rose* is classic Guild, available as wallpaper, fabric and accessories. In an Italian sitting room, the design is used to cover smart vintage chairs as well as easy curtains and, suddenly, the look moves away from nostalgia, to a new take on modern elegance.

Grandiflora Rose collection, Spring/Summer 2020.

company chronology

1970
Tricia Guild founds Designers Guild, whilst searching for textiles to decorate with. By re-colouring a collection of Indian hand block printed textiles, the first collection is born.

1972
The store on King's Road opens with the first collection of fabrics, also selling ceramics and furniture. It is more than just a store; it is an environment and a concept.

1976
Tricia Guild starts working with artists such as Kaffe Fassett, Lillian Delevoryas, Janice Tchalenko and others.

1982
Tricia Guild's first book is published – *Soft Furnishings.*

1986
Tricia Guild's brother Simon Jeffreys, who has a degree in Business Studies and Chartered Accountancy, joins the company in partnership with Tricia Guild as Chief Executive from the corporate finance division of international consultants Coopers & Lybrand.
Tricia Guild works with Howard Hodgkin on the celebrated enormous tulip fabrics *Large Flowers.*
Tricia Guild's second book is published – *Designing with Flowers.*

1988
Tricia Guild's third book is published – *Design and Detail.*

1989
The first Designers Guild office outside London opens in Munich.
The very first Designers Guild Kids collection is launched – *Merry-go-Round*; it is one of the first companies to design a collection exclusively for children's rooms.
Tricia Guild is awarded the Textile Institute Gold Medal for her outstanding contribution to international textiles, UK.
Tricia Guild's fourth book is published – *Design a Garden.*

1990
While the UK is in recession, Designers Guild focuses on expanding overseas.
Tricia Guild's fifth book is published – *New Soft Furnishings.*

1991
The company is awarded The Queen's Award for Export Achievement.

1992
The company is recognised and awarded with The Export Award for Smaller Businesses.
The first upholstery collection is launched.
Tricia Guild's sixth book is published – *Tricia Guild on Colour.*

1993
Tricia Guild is awarded an Honorary Fellowship from the Royal College of Art, London, as well as an Honorary Master of Arts Degree from Winchester School of Art, UK.
A new head office opens in Olaf Street, London.
The Paris office and showroom open.

1994
Designers Guild is a winner of the European Community Design prize.
Tricia Guild's seventh book is published – *Tricia Guild's Painted Country.*

1995
The launch of the Bed & Bath Division with a range of bedlinen, blankets and towels is recognised with the *Excellence de la Maison* award for bedlinen, by *Marie Claire Maison* magazine, France.

1996
The company is awarded The Queen's Award for Export Achievement.
A new 66,000 sq. ft Production and Distribution Centre in West London opens.
Tricia Guild's eighth book is published – *Tricia Guild in Town.*
The expansion of the flagship showrooms in London, which sell a total DG look with a showroom devoted entirely to fabrics, wallcoverings, furniture and paint, as well as the Homestore offering a dynamic and constantly changing range of essential items for the modern home, from furniture, bedlinen and bath accessories to ceramics and kitchenware.
The licensing division has become a growing part of the business, varying from upholstered furniture, a range of bedlinen, towels, blankets, rugs, personal organisers, luggage, carpets, gift-wrap and other paper products to an expanding collection of DG paint, all in perfect harmony with the fabric and wallpaper.
A softer more muted colour palette is introduced.

1997
The company is awarded the Home Tex Design Award, USA.
The Milan office opens.

1998
Tricia Guild's ninth book is published – *Cut Flowers.*
The first Designers Guild paint collection is launched.

1999
Tricia Guild is awarded an Honorary Degree of Doctor of Technology, from Loughborough University, UK.
Tricia Guild's tenth book is published – *White Hot.*

2001
The William Yeoward brand is added to the company's portfolio with the *Notebook* fabric collection.

2002
Tricia Guild's eleventh book is published – *Think Pink.*
Designers Guild is recognised with the Elle Decoration International Design Award for Best Fabric, Italy.

2003
The company is awarded Elle Decoration Best Wallpaper by *Elle Decoration USA.*
Designers Guild moves to brand new, purpose-built headquarters in London, W10.

2004
The launch of the first Designers Guild rug collection, to which new designs are added each season.
Tricia Guild's twelfth book is published – *Private View.*
The *Fragrant Home* collection launches with three scents: 'First Flower', 'Green Fig' and 'Waterleaf'.

2006
The Designers Guild Essentials division is created, comprising hundreds of plain and semi-plain fabric and wallpaper collections in a broad colour palette.
Tricia Guild's thirteenth book is published – *Pattern.*

2007

The *Homes & Gardens* Classic Design Award – Lifetime Achievement goes to Tricia Guild. The Paris showroom expands with a dedicated space for brands as well as Designers Guild collections.
The launch of the Milano Trevira CS weaves significantly expands the company's contract offer.
The 'Festival' and 'Hayward' furniture models are launched.
Tricia Guild's fourteenth book is published – *Flowers*.

2008

The Royal Collection of Fabrics and Wallcoverings launches – produced and distributed worldwide on behalf of the British Royal Household and inspired by the Royal Palaces, copyrighted 'Her Majesty Queen Elizabeth II'.
International launch events take place for The Royal Collection, held at The Queen's Gallery, Buckingham Palace and the Ambassador's Residence at the British Embassy, Paris.
Tricia Guild is awarded the OBE from HM The Queen for 'Services to Interior Design'.
The brand new UK website and online bed and bath shop is launched – the full Designers Guild lifestyle is now available to buy online within the UK.
Designers Guild is awarded 22nd place in the *Sunday Times* PwC Profit Track 100, of Britain's fastest growing privately owned firms.
Collaboration with Ladurée Paris with three specially designed DG boxes for their famous *macarons*.
Designers Guild is awarded the Microsoft prize for best use of technology.
The new Munich showroom opens in the heart of the city.

2009

Designers Guild is awarded a place for the second year running in the PwC Profit Track 100, for Britain's fastest growing privately owned firms.
New models are added to the growing furniture range – the 'Orbit' and 'Domino'.
The launch of Designers Guild Inc. to handle the bed, bath and accessory division in the USA.
The new USA online store launches, offering the full range of Designers Guild bedlinen and home accessories online throughout the USA.
'Portier' wallpaper is awarded Best Wallpaper by the UK *Homes & Gardens* Fabric Awards.

2010

Designers Guild is awarded the accolade 'Best British Brand' by *Elle Decoration* UK.
Tricia Guild's fifteenth book is published – *A Certain Style*.
New furniture models launch – the 'Julep', 'Cosmopolitan', 'Gibson', 'Soho' and 'Brooklyn'
The first Homestore away from King's Road opens on Marylebone High Street in April 2010.

2011

Designers Guild voted 'Best British Brand' for the second consecutive year by readers of *Elle Decoration* UK.
Iconic international luxury brand Christian Lacroix Maison launches its first collection for the home under licence to Designers Guild – 'Arles' fabrics and wallpapers, followed by home accessories in autumn 2011.
The 'Spin' sofa and chair are added to Designers Guild's extensive furniture portfolio.

The Howard Hodgkin collection is launched with four designs and accessories.

2012.

Christian Lacroix 'Vuelta' design from the *Arles* collection is awarded 'Best Fabric' at the *Elle Decoration* International Design Awards (EDIDAs).
Five new furniture models are added to the range: 'Ellipse', 'Button', 'Stitch', 'Flute' and 'Harper'.
A special cushion is designed to commemorate the Diamond Jubilee of Queen Elizabeth II.
Designers Guild for the Table launches with a collection of contemporary tableware, all uniquely designed by Tricia Guild.

2013

The 'Savine' design is awarded 'Best Wallpaper' by *Homes & Gardens* Fabric Awards, UK.
Tricia Guild publishes new book, her sixteenth to date – *Colour Deconstructed* – in nine languages.
The launch of the Designers Guild blog.
Designers Guild joins social media through Facebook, Twitter, Instagram and Pinterest.

2014

A brand new 80,000 sq. ft logistics and distribution warehouse opens in West London.
An upgraded and highly functional website is launched.
A new paint range is launched with a collection of 154 colours.
Designers Guild exhibits for the first time at Design Junction, London.

2015

May sees the launch of a dramatic new floral collection with Italian tile brand Bisazza, featuring three romantic, large-scale designs adapted from Designers Guild's own hand-painted floral patterns.
In October the DG online store launches in France.
The first online furniture collection, 'The Bedroom Edit', is launched in November through the UK online shop.

2016

A brand new showroom opens in the heart of the Paris design district.
Online stores in France and Spain are launched.

2017

Tricia Guild publishes her seventeenth book, *Paint Box*, demystifying the process of decorating with colours.

2018

New retail space dedicated to wallpaper and paint opens on King's Road, joining the existing Homestore and Showroom.

2019

Collaboration with Cappellini furniture.
Publication of Tricia Guild's eighteenth book – *In My View*.

2020

Designers Guild celebrates its fiftieth anniversary with an exhibition at the Fashion and Textile Museum, London.

collections chronology

1975
Village

1976
Geranium

1977
Poppy Vase

1978
Bean, Daisy

1979
Watercolour, Splatter

1980
Mainstream, Tricia Guild Soft Furnishings

1982
Rags, Tatters

1983
Angles, Moonshine, Rough Diamond, Doubleglaze

1984
Natural Classics, Anemone, Cotton Twist

1985
Paper Roses, Chintz Classics, Trees, Blossom, Gardenia, Textures, Flowers

1986
Wildflower, Howard Hodgkin, Ornamental Garden, Watergarden, Waterleaf

1987
Filigree, Spring Flower, Plains, Grandiflora, Gesso

1988
Maypole, Tapisserie, Tapestry Leaves, Cassia, Damas Fleuri, Filigrana

1989
Oriental Flowers, Impressions du Midi, Castellane, Il Veneto, Vicenza, Torcello
First Designers Guild Kids collection launched: *Merry-go-Round*

1990
Summer House, Passariano, Bokhara, Kashgar, Astrakhan

1991
Mardi Gras, Marquetry, Abracadabra, Pergamena, Chazelles, Tarsus, Nantua, Cartiglio, Cushma Trimmings, Vinchina Cushions, Firefly
First trimmings collection launched: *Cushma*

1992
Still Life, The Melon Patch, Harvest, Orissa, Jalna, Japonica, Katibo, Tindall, Amhara
First upholstery collection launched: the *Canonbury* collection

1993
Santa Margherita, Mahé, Puntino, Kusumam, Jalapuri, Lalitha, Kalamkari

1994
Toy Box, Gouache, Phulkari, Sujani, Kaffe's Pots and new upholstery

1995
Mei P'ing, Milford, Tullow, Tirupati, Sakumari, Saffa, Kashipur, Orientalis, Jhati, Tianjun

1996
Isika, Hopscotch, Pushpa, Dalton, Marquetry II, Brera, Oola, Karahana, Artemisia, Palazzo, Ryoshi, Diagonale, Palatino, Borghese, Vercelli

1997
Salsa, Granita, Bakhia, Ottavia, Emerson, Arklow, Patadar, Allerby, Rajkot, Tamarind, Ashrafi, Nyamati, Jalaja
Table linen launched

1998
Tiddlywink, Damascena, Solferino, Manjeri, Bergamo, Candassa, Tassi, Tafta, Mandriola, Torridon
Paint collection launched

1999
Quanjin, Broadcloth, Kells, Passiflora, Kutru Trimmings, Peshkir, Canareggio, Batiste, Orani, Velluto, Veryan
Personal Organisers collection launched

2000
La Désirade, Bindi, Cats Chorus, Mistral, Brera, Kepala, Makasar, Fiesole, Parioli, Serang
New luggage range launched
New rug range launched
Mail order catalogue 'At Home' launched
Emily Todhunter brand launched: *Tuileries Fabrics and Wallpapers*

2001
Pontalba Fabrics and Wallpapers, Izapa, Estrêla, On Your Marks, Zandanechi, Colour Book, Cozenza, Nurata
New furniture designs launched
William Yeoward brand launched: *Notebook*
Two new mail order catalogues: 'At Home' and 'Designers Guild Kids'
New carpets and tufted rugs
Table linen

2002
Cristobal Fabrics and Wallpapers, Habanera, Tejeda, Over the Moon, Inessa, Pavlovsk, Trezzini
Second collection of William Yeoward fabric and wallpaper: *Sketchbook*

2003
Imari, Shibori, Masuda, Mezzola Stripe, China Rose, Saraceno, Shibori, Rosalina

2004
Mirabeau, Rousillon, Veran, Bokashi Outdoor, Hide & Seek, Companions, Chinon, Naturally, New Paint Collection, Rugs, Amaranth, Ombrione, Coromandel, Varese, Mezzola Twill and Tweed, Arezzo, Mantova, Mezzola Maggiore, Breganze
Fragrant Home collection launched with three scents: 'First flower', 'Green Fig' and 'Waterleaf'

2005
Cherry Orchard Fabric and Wallpaper, Cherry Orchard Braids, Merindol, Banon Printed Stripes, Mezzola Bellusco, Cabannes Outdoor
Samarkand, Brocatelle, Bukhara Flock, Ruzzini, Focsari,, Callian, Pallanza and *Bukhara Wallpapers*
New *Fragrant Home* products: 'Shanghai Rose' and 'Summer Vine'

2006
Gran Paradiso, Panama, Arlanza, Najasa, Catalan, Portobello, Etoile, Conway and *Brera II*
Sarafan, Coromandel, Anastasia, Monplaisir, Mezzola Repino, Indian Summer Archive Collection, William Yeoward *Ranakpur Collection*
Designers Guild Essentials division launched – fabric and wallpaper collections featuring plain and semi-plain designs in a broad colour palette

2007
Oriental Garden prints and wallcoverings, *Kibushi, Kashima*
Essentials: *Shima, Hoxton, Rossano, Ribera, Ferrara Trevira CS, Kaya, Amalienborg, Quarenghi Taillandier, Kasimir, Mezzola/Mezzola Lusso, Brescia, Bamberg*
Limited-edition candles *Peony* and *Limeflower, Capucheen* and *Guirlande*

2008
Florimund Prints and Wallcoverings, Racine, Correze, Roquelaire, Arzino, Tsuga Essentials (new colourways), *Satinato Essentials, Primrose Hill Prints and Wallpapers, Orsetti Trimmings*, William Yeoward *Delacroix*
Arabella Prints and Wallcoverings, Monteverdi, Ariana, Alisede, Ruggiero, Chambord; and *Milano Trevira CS* weaves significantly expands the company's contract offerings
'Festival' and 'Hayward' furniture models launched
'Giacosa' candle launched
The Royal Collection of Fabrics and Wallcoverings, launched, produced and distributed worldwide on behalf of the British Royal Household and inspired by the Royal Palaces, with worldwide launch events at The Queen's Gallery, Buckingham Palace and in the Ambassador's Residence at the British Embassy in Paris – all copyrighted 'Her Majesty Queen Elizabeth II'

2009

Whitewell Prints and Wallcoverings, *Tsuga*, *Adelphi*, *Maitland*, *Manhattan*, *Rinzu*, *Orsetti*, *Bilbao* and *Bassano*, William Yeoward *Aurelie Darly Prints and Wallpapers*, *Roumier*, *Valadier*, *Quinto* Designers Guild Essentials: *Cali*, *Cascina*, *Black and White Essentials* and *Carlu Wallpapers* The second Royal Collection of Fabrics and Wallpapers – *Savigny* The launch of a new FR collection *Santiago* New USA online shop launched New furniture models launched – the 'Orbit' and 'Domino' New larger three-wick candle 'Darly' is added to the *Fragrant Home* range

2010

Pavilion, *Nabucco*, *Cassan*, *Nantucket*, *Barcelona*, *Tiana Outdoor* Designers Guild Essentials Collections: *Brera Alta*, *Brera Lino*, *Kellas* and *Tiber*, *Nash Grasscloth*, William Yeoward's *Aranjasa* *Zephirine Prints*, *Zephirine Wallcoverings*, *Bernardini*, *Trevelyan*, *Cecilia Trevira Moray Essentials*, *Brenan Essentials*, *Arno Essentials*, *Nabucco Essentials*, The Royal Collection of Fabrics and Wallpapers: *Campanula* New furniture models launched at Maison et Objet in Paris: the 'Julep', 'Cosmopolitan', 'Gibson', 'Soho' and 'Brooklyn'

2011

Sofienberg Prints and Linnaeus Wallcoverings, *Borgholm Weaves*, *Trasimeno Weaves*, *Lauzon wide-width Sheers* Designers Guild Unlimited Collections: *Miami*, *Deltona* and *Oxbridge* Designers Guild Essentials: *Brera Rigato*, *Allia*, *Salso*, *Piave* and *Mezzola* (relaunched with new colourways) New Designers Guild Kids Collection: *Around the World Prints and Wallpapers* William Yeoward *Polperro* The iconic international luxury brand Christian Lacroix launches its first

Collection for the Home under licence to Designers Guild – *Arles* Launch of Howard Hodgkin collection with four designs and accessories

2012

Designers Guild: *Kimono Blossom*, *Kasuri*, *Perreau* and *Mazan* Designers Guild Unlimited: *Country*, *Havana*, *Brera* and *Fleuve* Designers Guild Essentials: *Brera Quadretto*, *Tickings*, *Salerno* and *Aviano* Five new furniture models launched: 'Ellipse', 'Button', 'Stitch', 'Flute' and 'Harper' William Yeoward launches two new collections: *Exmere* and *Manton*, as well as new accessories Christian Lacroix Maison for Designers Guild launches 'Air de Paris' fabrics, wallpapers and accessories New accessories added to The Royal Collection range for Spring 2012, including a special cushion to commemorate the Diamond Jubilee of Her Majesty Queen Elizabeth II *Pavonia* and *Castellani*, *Castellani Moselle* Designers Guild Essentials: *Torgiano*, *Chinon*, *Sicilia* and *Arizona* The Royal Collection of Fabrics and Wallpapers: *Elizabeth* New accessories for Christian Lacroix Maison

2013

Designers Guild: *Seraphina*, *Contarini*, *Padua*, *Savine* and *Canossa Trevira* Designers Guild Unlimited: *Lavandou* Designers Guild Essentials: *Iona*, *Sloane* and *Cara* William Yeoward launches two new collections: *Astasia Prints* and *Monsoreto Weaves*, as well as new accessories Christian Lacroix Maison for Designers Guild launches fabrics, wallpapers and accessories: *Carnets Andalous Astrkahan Prints and Silks*, *Alexandria*, *Savine*, *Zambelli*, *Zetani* Essentials Collections – *Morvern*, *Bressia*, *Cassia*, *Mezzola Alta*

2014

For Designers Guild: *Kaori* and *Amlapura Prints*, *Savio Weaves*, *Moselle Vegetale Weaves*, *Surabaya Wallpapers*, *Saraille wide-width Linens* Essentials: *Naturally V*, *Naturally VI*, *Brera Lino*, *Bolsena* and *Lucente FR* For Christian Lacroix Maison: *Belle Rives* Designers Guild Autumn/Winter 2014: *Madhuri*, *Borati*, *Indupala*, *Amaya*, *Sukumala*, *Palasini* Designers Guild Autumn/Winter 2014 Essentials: *Mesilla*, *Kalahari*, *Ishida*, *Satinato II*, *FR Aquarelle* The Royal Collection: *St James's Fabric Collection* William Yeoward: *Marlena*, *Alberesque*, *Library* Christian Lacroix Maison: new accessories

2015

For Designers Guild: *Shanghai Garden Prints and Wallpapers*, *Aurelia* and *Mirafiori* Essentials: *Brera Rigato II*, *Manzoni*, *Tiber II* For Christian Lacroix Maison: *Nouvelles Mondes*, and *Atelier Carmargue* Mid Season – April 2015 For Designers Guild: *Orangerie II Prints*, *The Edit... Patterned Wallcoverings Volume I* and *The Edit... Plain and Textured Wallcoverings Volume I* Autumn/Winter 2015 For Designers Guild: *Caprifoglio Prints and Wallpapers*, *Boratti*, *Pugin*, *Aalter*, *Portico*, *Tweed FR Fabrics*, *Maggia*, *Bilbao II*, *Zaragoza*, *Mavone*, *Metallo* For The Royal Collection: *Buckingham Fabrics and Wallpapers*, *Palace Damasks* For William Yeoward: *Indigo bleu Fabric*

2016

For Designers Guild: *Couture Rose* and *Marquisette* wallpapers and *Colonnade Fabrics* and *Greycloth Fabrics* Essentials: *Canvas*, *Rothesay*, *Conway*, *Riveau*, *Cassano* For Christian Lacroix Maison: *Incroyables et Merveilleuses Fabrics and Wallpapers* Autumn/Winter 2016 For Designers Guild: *Jardins Des Plantes Prints and Wallpapers*, *Parchment*

Wallpapers, *Forsyth*, *Majella Pavia Nevada Scala Trevellas*, *Canzo*, *Monza* For William Yeoward: *Rufolo* and *Torca*

2017

For Designers Guild: *Majolica Fabrics and Wallpaper*, *Murrine*, *Palasari* Essentials: *Brera Lino III*, *Matara*, *Mirissa*, *Ampara* For Christian Lacroix: *Au Thèâtre Ce Soir Fabric and Wallpaper*, *Au Thèâtre Ce Soir* Autumn/Winter 2017 For Designers Guild: *Tulipa Stellata Fabrics and Wallpapers*, *Casablanca*, *Casablanca Textured Wallpapers*, *Bellavista Berwick* Essentials: *Varese II*, *Tammaro*, *Sesia*, *Keswick*, *Mineral Weaves*, *Contract Essentials II* For William Yeoward: *Pellenport*, *Larkin*, *Philippine*

2018

For Designers Guild: *Giardino Segreto*, *Carlotta*, *Chareau*, *Savoie*, *Mandora* Essentials: *Trentino FR*, *Trentino Stretto*, *Vicenza*, *Madrid*, *Brera Moda*, *Kumana*, *Lauziere* For Christian Lacroix: *Histoires Naturelles Fabrics and Wallpapers* John Derian By Designers Guild: *Picture Book Fabrics and Wallpapers* Autumn/Winter 2018 For Designers Guild: *Jaipur Rose Chandigarh*, *Zardozi Fabric and Wallpapers* Essentials: *Calozzo*, *Birkett*, *Melton* For William Yeoward: *Delcia*, *Library III*

2019

For Designers Guild: *Veronese*, *Palladio*, *Palme Botanique*, *Fortezza*, *Foscari Fresco* Essentials: *Anshu*, *Valloire*, *Lisbon*, *Porto* For Christian Lacroix: *Paradis Barbares Fabrics and Wallpaper* For Ralph Lauren: *Signature Artisan Loft*, *Signature Islesboro* John Derian by Designers Guild: *Picture Book II* Autumn/Winter 2019 For Designers Guild: *Le Poème De Fleurs Fabrics*, *Fitzrovia*, *Scenes & Murals* Essentials: *Matara II*, *Opera Easyclean*, *Canezza*, *Velluto* For William Yeoward: *Florian*

acknowledgements

I would like to thank the Designers Guild team past and present who have made an invaluable contribution towards making the company what it is today.

My special thanks go to my brother Simon Jeffreys CEO, whose contribution has ensured our continued success, and to the DG Board of Directors – Michael Findlay, Colin Fraser and Margaret Romanski – and to our Senior Managers. They have looked after and cared for every aspect of the company as it has developed and as it continues to progress.

I am very fortunate to work with such an amazing group of like-minded people: my brilliant Design Studio, including Sandii Dwyer, Charlotte Dunker, Sophie Thorne and Esme Tustin; and the Creative, Product Development and Press teams. Thank you for living and breathing DG.

Remembering Valerie Roy's stunning designs.

I would particularly like to acknowledge and thank the following members of the team who have made this book and exhibition possible: Chloe Bawden, Blythe Bruckner, Eden Calder, Julian Cloke, Charlotte Clowes, Claire FitzPatrick, Jo Foster, Jenny Hamblin, Jasmine Hussona, Georgia Loveridge, Tamzin Munro, Tanja Sharp, Georgia Wagner, Sara Weavers, Jo Willer and last, but certainly not least, Amanda Back, who has written the text for this book.

We have had some fantastic help with delving into the last 50 years of DG, especially from Catherine de Chabeneix, who has located much of the imagery. I have been fortunate to work with many hugely talented photographers such as Gilles de Chabeneix, Ben Edwards, James Merrell, David Montgomery, Bruce Wolf and Polly Wreford.

Louise Brody has designed this book with an expert eye, and has been a pleasure to work with, as have the publishers at ACC Art Books.

And finally, of course, I would like to express my wholehearted gratitude to the brilliant team at the Fashion and Textile Museum: Dennis Nothdruft, Melissa French and Bethan Ojari.

photo credits

All photographs by **James Merrell** except:

Tricia Guild: p.7/8 top row: 2nd,3rd, 6th, 7th from left, bottom row: 2nd, 5th from left; p.10 2nd from top, 4th from top; p.11 all images; p.12/13 top row: 1st, 3rd, 4th, 7th from left, middle row: 2nd, 3rd, 4th, 6th, 7th from left, bottom row: 1st, 2nd, 3rd, 4th from left; p.28 all images; p.30 3rd, 4th from top; p.32 bottom left, bottom right; p.33 middle row, middle; p.34 middle row, middle, right; p.42; p.76 2nd, 3rd, 4th from left; p.118 2nd, 3rd, 4th from left; p.154; p.192 2nd, 3rd, 4th from left

© René Burri/Magnum photos. © Barragan Foundation / DACS 2019: p.10 3rd from top

Gilles de Chabaneix: p.36 top row: 2nd from left; p.38 left; p.40; p.44 bottom row: 1st from left, 2nd from left, top row: 1st from left, 2nd from left, 3rd from left; p.45; p.46 top left, bottom left; p.48 top left; p.50; p.51; p.52 top left; p.54; p.116; p.118 left; p.120; p.156 bottom left, bottom right

Ben Edwards: p.22 2nd from top, 3rd from top; p.23; p.25 4th row: 1st from left, 3rd from left

Dustin Hare: p.243

Anthony Harvey/Shutterstock: p.10 top

David Montgomery: p.17 bottom; p.18 2nd from bottom; p.20 2nd from bottom; p.33 top row, 1st from left, 3rd row 1st from left; p.36 top row, 1st from left; p.74; p.75 top, 2nd from top, 3rd from top; p.78 top left, top right; p.117 2nd from top; p.156 bottom middle; p.224 top left, bottom right; p.225 top right; p.226 bottom right; p.227 top right

Bruce Wolf: p16; p17

Polly Wreford: p.36 top row, 3rd from left, 2nd row all; p.37 top row 1st from left, 2nd row 1st from left, 3rd row 2nd from left; p.122 top row, middle

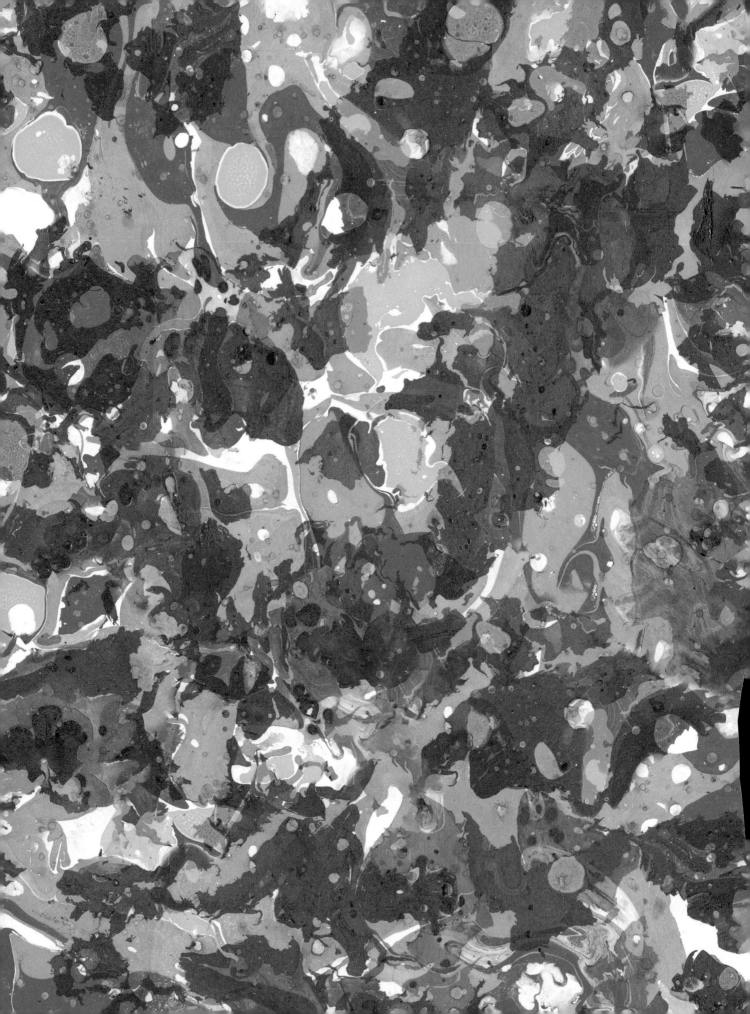